Fall Shakes
to Harvest Bakes

by **Marilyn LaPenta**

Consultant:
Mandi Pek, MS, RD, CSP, CDN

BEARPORT
PUBLISHING

NEW YORK, NEW YORK

Credits

All food illustrations by Kim Jones

Publisher: Kenn Goin
Editor: Joy Bean
Creative Director: Spencer Brinker
Design: Debrah Kaiser

Library of Congress Cataloging-in-Publication Data

La Penta, Marilyn.
   Fall shakes to harvest bakes / by Marilyn LaPenta ; consultant: Mandi Pek, MS, RD, CSP, CDN.
      pages cm. — (Yummy tummy recipes: seasons)
   Includes bibliographical references and index.
   ISBN 978-1-61772-742-9 (library binding) — ISBN 1-61772-742-3 (library binding)
   1. Cooking—Juvenile literature. 2. Seasonal cooking—Juvenile literature. I. Title.
   TX652.5.L375 2013
   641.5'64—dc23
                          2012033940

For more information, write to Bearport Publishing Company, Inc., 45 West 21st Street, Suite 3B, New York, New York, 10010. Printed in the United States of America.

10 9 8 7 6 5 4 3 2 1

Contents

Making Healthy Fall Treats

Get ready to make some yummy fall treats! All of the delicious creations in *Fall Shakes to Harvest Bakes* include the fresh **produce** of the season. Always try to buy fruits and vegetables for these recipes at farmers' markets or small family farms. The produce at these places has often just been picked and usually has more nutritional value and flavor than fruits and vegetables shipped long distances.

The great thing about making your own food is that you know exactly what goes into it. Many **pre-made** foods that you buy in grocery stores have ingredients to **preserve** them. These preservatives are not always good for your body. Pre-made foods also often have too much fat, sugar, and salt to be healthy. While all the recipes in this book call for nutritious ingredients, you can make them even healthier by using the ideas on page 22.

Getting Started

Use these cooking tips and safety and tool guidelines to make the best shakes and baked goods you've ever tasted.

Tips

Here are a few tips to get your cooking off to a great start.

- Quickly check out the Prep Time, Cooking Time, Tools, and Servings information at the top of each recipe. It will tell you how long the recipe takes to prepare, the tools you'll need, and the number of people the recipe serves.

- Once you pick a recipe, set out the tools and ingredients that you will need on your worktable.

- Before and after cooking, wash your hands well with warm soapy water to kill any germs.

- Wash fruits and vegetables, as appropriate, to get rid of any dirt and chemicals.

- Put on an apron or smock to protect your clothes.

- Roll up long shirtsleeves to keep them clean.

- Tie back long hair or cover it to keep it out of the food.

- *Very Important:* Keep the adults happy by cleaning up the kitchen when you've finished cooking.

PREP TIME   **COOKING TIME**   **TOOLS**   **SERVINGS**   **INGREDIENTS**   **RECIPE**

5 Minutes Prep Time   **2** Hours Cooking Time   Tools   **6** Servings

Ingredients

2 medium apples   2 tablespoons cinnamon

Steps

1. **Preheat** the oven to 225°F.
2. Peel the apple. Cut out the **core** and discard. Ask an adult to cut the apple into thin slices (about ⅛ inch thick) with the knife on the cutting board.
3. Line the baking sheet with parchment paper.
4. Put the apple slices on the parchment paper.
5. Sprinkle cinnamon on the apples.
6. Bake in the oven for 1½ to 2 hours. After 1 hour, flip the apples over with the spatula, holding the baking sheet still with the pot holder. Check every 15 minutes after flipping. (Thinner slices will bake more quickly than thicker ones.)
7. Once the slices look nice and crispy, carefully remove the baking sheet from the oven with the pot holder.
8. Let the apple rings cool and enjoy. The slices will keep in an airtight container for a week.

The largest apple ever picked was 3 pounds. That is the same weight as a ⅓ gallon of milk.

Be Safe

Keep these safety tips in mind while you are in the kitchen.

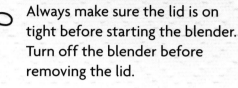

🥄 Ask an adult for help when cutting, peeling, or grating any food.

🥄 Make sure an adult is present when using the blender, oven, or stovetop.

🥄 Make sure the blender is turned off before adding ingredients.

🥄 Never plug or unplug a blender with wet hands.

🥄 Never stick your hands inside a blender while it is plugged in.

🥄 Always make sure the lid is on tight before starting the blender. Turn off the blender before removing the lid.

🥄 Always use pot holders when removing hot pans from the oven.

Tools You Need

Here's a guide to the tools you will need to make the various recipes in this book.

Mixing spoon

Spoon

Fork

Knife

Ladle

Apple or vegetable peeler

Spatula

Straw

Measuring spoons

Measuring cups

Can opener

Small bowl

Medium mixing bowl

Large mixing bowl

Plate

Medium glass, 12 ounces

Mug

Ice cube tray

Cutting board

Pot holders

Plastic bag

Parchment paper

Salad spinner

Colander

Wire rack

Medium pot

Small frying pan

Blender

Baking sheet with sides

Muffin tin

Baking sheet without sides

Electric mixer

Stovetop

Oven

Refrigerator

Microwave

7

Pumpkin Spice Smoothie

5
Minutes
Prep Time

 Tools

1
Serving

Ingredients

½ cup canned pumpkin

1 cup nondairy milk
(unsweetened almond
milk works well)

1 frozen banana, peeled

1 teaspoon maple syrup

½ teaspoon pure vanilla
extract

¼ teaspoon cinnamon

¼ teaspoon nutmeg (or
½ teaspoon pumpkin
pie spice instead of
cinnamon and nutmeg)

Extra cinnamon for
decoration

Steps

1. Ask an adult to open the can of pumpkin.

2. Put the nondairy milk, pumpkin, banana, maple syrup, vanilla extract, cinnamon, and nutmeg in the blender.

3. **Blend** on high for 1 minute or until smooth.

4. Pour the mixture into a glass.

5. Sprinkle with cinnamon.

Health Tip

This smoothie is **vegan, gluten free, dairy free,** yeast free, and corn free.

Pumpkins aren't just for eating.
Native Americans flattened
strips of pumpkin, dried them,
and made them into mats.

8

Apple Shake

Tools

Ingredients

1 large apple

1 frozen banana, peeled

2 cups **low-fat** milk

6 ice cubes

2 teaspoons cinnamon

Steps

1. With the help of an adult, peel the apple, cut out the **core**, and discard it. Place the apple on the cutting board. Use the knife to slice 4 2-inch-long pieces off the apple. Then cut the remaining apple into bite-size pieces.

2. Put the apple pieces, the peeled banana, and ½ cup of milk into the blender. **Blend** on high for 40 seconds or until **creamy**.

3. Gradually add the rest of the milk and ice and blend on high until **foamy**, about 1 minute.

4. Pour the mixture into two glasses.

5. Sprinkle with cinnamon.

6. Float 2 apple slices in each glass for decoration.

John Chapman was the real name of Johnny Appleseed, who was born on September 26, 1774. He helped spread apples across America by planting thousands of acres of apple trees across the country.

Health Tip

One apple has lots of **fiber** and only 90 to 95 **calories**. Most of the fiber is in the skin—so don't peel apples before eating them.

9

Grape Surprise Fizzle

2 Minutes Prep Time*

Tools

2 Servings

Plus 3 Hours Freezer Time

Ingredients

6 grapes (red or green)

Water

⅔ cup grape juice

16 ounces seltzer

Steps

1. Wash the grapes in the colander. Put one grape in 6 of the compartments in the ice cube tray. Fill the 6 compartments that have a grape in them with water and put in the freezer.

2. Wait until the ice is frozen, about 3 hours.

3. Put 3 ice cubes in each glass.

4. Pour ⅓ cup of grape juice into each glass.

5. Pour seltzer in each glass until full. Watch the juice fizzle!

6. Sip through a fun straw.

Grapes are 80 percent water, but when they are turned into raisins, the water content is just 15 percent.

Health Tip

Grapes stay fresh for about 2 to 3 days in the refrigerator when stored in a plastic bag or a covered container and taste best when slightly chilled.

Seltzer

Mulled Apple Cider

5 Minutes Prep Time

30 Minutes Cooking Time

Tools

8 Servings

Ingredients

8 cups apple cider

1 apple

6 cloves

12 sticks cinnamon

2 strips orange rind, 2–3 inches long

Steps

1. Put the cider in a medium-size pot on the stovetop.

2. Peel the apple. Then ask an adult to use the knife to slice it into 1-inch-long pieces on the cutting board. Throw out the **core**.

3. Add the apple pieces to the pot.

4. Add the cloves, 4 cinnamon sticks, and the orange strips to the pot.

5. Cook the mixture over medium heat until it just starts to bubble, then reduce to low heat and **simmer** gently for 30 minutes.

6. With an adult's help, use the pot holders to carefully move the pot next to the sink. Use a ladle to spoon the cider from the pot into a small strainer that has been placed over a mug. Fill the other mugs with cider in the same way.

7. Add a cinnamon stick to each mug.

Fifty percent of the apples grown in America are eaten fresh. The average American eats 20 to 25 pounds of apples every year.

Health Tip

A single apple supplies about a quarter of your day's vitamin C needs.

11

Popcorn Trail Mix

5 Minutes Prep Time

Tools

4 Servings

Ingredients

4 cups popped popcorn

½ cup peanut butter chips

½ cup roasted peanuts (or your favorite nut)

½ cup dried cranberries or raisins

¼ cup seeds (pumpkin or sunflower)

Have fun creating your own mix. Add any of your favorite treats to the mix, such as: shredded coconut, goldfish crackers, mini pretzels, mini cheese crackers, chocolate chips, crumpled kale chips, banana chips or other dried fruit.

Steps

1 Put popped popcorn in a plastic bag.

2 Add the peanut butter chips, peanuts, dried cranberries, and seeds.

3 Shake the bag to mix.

4 Pour the mix into the bowl and enjoy!

If you made a trail of popcorn from New York City to Los Angeles, you would need more than 352,028,160 popped kernels.

Light Pumpkin Mousse

10 Minutes Prep Time*

Tools

4 Servings

* Plus 2 Hours to Chill

Health Tip

Pumpkins are very low in **calories**, just 26 per 3½ ounces. They are a rich source of **vitamins**, **minerals**, and **fiber**.

Ingredients

8 ounces canned pumpkin

1 cup skim or **low-fat** milk

¼ teaspoon nutmeg

¼ teaspoon cinnamon

1 small package instant sugar-free vanilla pudding

1 cup fat-free whipped cream

Steps

1. Ask an adult to open the can of pumpkin.

2. Combine the pumpkin, milk, nutmeg, and cinnamon in the medium mixing bowl.

3. Mix with the spoon until the mixture is smooth.

4. Add in the pudding mix and **beat** with the electric mixer for 1 to 2 minutes.

5. With the spoon, **fold** in the whipped cream until well blended.

6. Spoon the mixture into the small bowls and chill in the refrigerator for 1 to 2 hours before serving.

The word pumpkin is from the Greek word pepon, which means "large melon." The French changed the word to pompon, and the English changed it to pumpion. American colonists later called it pumpkin.

13

Baked Apple Rings

5 Minutes Prep Time

2 Hours Cooking Time

Tools

6 Servings

Ingredients

2 medium apples   2 tablespoons cinnamon

Steps

1. **Preheat** the oven to 225°F.

2. Peel each apple. Cut out the **core** and discard. Ask an adult to use the knife to cut the apple into thin slices (about ⅛ inch thick) on the cutting board.

3. Line the baking sheet with the parchment paper.

4. Put the apple slices on the parchment paper.

5. Sprinkle cinnamon on the apples.

6. Bake in the oven for 1 ½ to 2 hours. After 1 hour, flip the apples over with the spatula, holding the baking sheet still with the pot holder. Check every 15 minutes after flipping. (Thinner slices will bake more quickly than thicker ones.)

7. Once the slices look nice and crispy, carefully remove the baking sheet from the oven with the pot holder.

8. Let the apple rings cool and enjoy. The slices will keep in an airtight container for a week.

Cinnamon

The largest apple ever picked was 3 pounds. That is the same weight as a ½ gallon of milk.

Cranberry Nut Bars

Health Tip

Cranberries are full of **antioxidants**, which protect the cells in our bodies from damage.

10 Minutes Prep Time

20 Minutes Cooking Time

Tools

Makes 20 Bars

Ingredients

Cooking spray

3 cups old-fashioned oats (or mix quick oats and old-fashioned)

½ cup **hulled** pumpkin seeds

½ cup slivered almonds

1 cup mixed nuts of your choice

1 cup dried cranberries

14-ounce can sweetened condensed milk

Steps

1. **Preheat** the oven to 350°F. Line the baking sheet with parchment paper, with about 1 inch of paper left on each side for "handles." Spray the paper lightly with cooking spray.

2. Put the oats, seeds, nuts, and cranberries in the bowl and mix with the spoon.

3. Ask an adult to open the can of condensed milk. Add the milk to the bowl and stir with the spoon until well blended.

4. Pour the mixture onto the the parchment-lined baking sheet. Spread it out to the sides and corners with the spoon.

5. Bake for 20 minutes for chewy bars or 25 minutes for crunchy bars.

6. Carefully remove the baking sheet from the oven with the pot holders. Allow it to cool for 5 minutes.

7. Lift the baked mixture out of the baking sheet using the edges of the parchment paper. Cut it into bars.

Native Americans believed cranberries had medicinal value and used them to draw poison from arrow wounds.

Kale Chips

10 Minutes Prep Time

20 Minutes Cooking Time

Tools

6 Servings

Ingredients

1 bunch kale

2 tablespoons light olive oil

Salt to taste

Pepper to taste

Steps

1. **Preheat** the oven to 325°F.

2. Carefully tear the kale leaves off the stems.

3. Rinse the leaves and put them in the salad spinner to dry (or pat the leaves dry between two paper towels).

4. Rip the kale leaves into bite-size pieces (about 2 inches).

5. Put the kale pieces in the bowl and sprinkle them with olive oil. Toss the pieces with your fingers to mix in the olive oil.

6. Place the leaves, curly side down, on the baking sheet and sprinkle with salt and pepper to taste.

7. Bake for 20 minutes or until the edges are light brown. (If you like them crispy, bake them until they are fully brown.)

8. Carefully remove the baking sheet from the oven with the pot holders. Let the chips cool for 1 minute.

9. The kale pieces are fragile, so remove them from the baking sheet carefully and put them on the plate.

Health Tip

Kale chips are a very healthy snack because kale's nutrition increases when it is cooked.

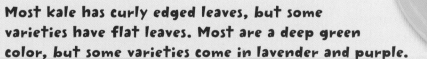

Most kale has curly edged leaves, but some varieties have flat leaves. Most are a deep green color, but some varieties come in lavender and purple.

Baked Pumpkin Seeds

 20 Minutes Prep Time*

 **1** Hour Cooking Time

Tools

Serves a Group

* Plus 2 Days Soaking and Drying Time

Ingredients

Pumpkin seeds from a fresh pumpkin

Warm water

2–3 tablespoons olive oil or coconut oil

Salt

If desired, also use other spices—pumpkin pie spice, cinnamon, nutmeg, garlic powder

Steps

1. Rinse the seeds in the colander. Use your fingers to remove all the orange pulp.

2. Put the seeds in the bowl. Cover them with warm water. For each cup of seeds, add ¼ cup of salt.

3. Allow the seeds to sit in the water for 24 hours.

4. Use the colander to drain the water from the seeds. Lay them out on the baking sheet to dry for 8 hours.

5. **Preheat** the oven to 300°F.

6. Toss the seeds with the oil and sprinkle with salt and any other spices you like.

7. **Roast** the seeds in the oven for one hour, tossing them every 15 to 20 minutes.

8. Cool before storing and eating.

Pumpkin seeds are also called pepitas.

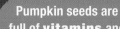

Sweet Potatoes with Black Bean Topping

25
Minutes
Total Prep
Time

Tools

2-4
Servings

Ingredients

2 medium sweet potatoes or yams

1 ½ tablespoons olive oil

2 tablespoons chopped green pepper

1 tablespoon chopped hot pepper

1 clove garlic, peeled and minced

2 tablespoons chopped onion

1 ½ cups cooked black beans, drained

1 cup salsa

1 teaspoon cumin

¼ teaspoon cilantro, if desired

¼ teaspoon salt

Pinch black pepper

Steps

1. Rinse the sweet potatoes. Poke them with the fork several times on both sides. Then cook them for about 7 minutes in the microwave. They are done when soft. Let them cool for a few minutes.

2. In the frying pan, heat the olive oil over medium heat on the stovetop. Then add the green pepper, hot pepper, garlic, and onion, and **sauté** for 5 minutes.

3. Drain the beans in the colander and then add them, along with the salsa, to the frying pan.

4. Add the cumin, cilantro, salt, and pepper and stir with the spoon until heated through, about 10 minutes.

5. Put the potatoes on the plates. Slice them in half lengthwise and put the bean mixture on top of each one.

Health Tip

Sweet potatoes are high in iron, magnesium, and **vitamins** A, B, C, and D.

Sweet potatoes and yams are often confused because they look alike, but they are not related. Yams have a shaggy skin while sweet potatoes have smooth skin.

Salsa

Black Beans organic

Pumpkin Muffins

10 Minutes Prep Time

25–40 Minutes Cooking Time

Tools

12–15 Muffins or 24 Mini Muffins

Ingredients

Cooking spray

1 cup canned pumpkin

¾ cup honey

2 eggs

½ teaspoon baking soda

1 teaspoon baking powder

½ teaspoon salt

1 ½ teaspoons pumpkin pie spice (or nutmeg and cinnamon)

1 ⅔ cups whole wheat flour

½ cup melted butter or coconut oil

¼ cup cold water

Optional: ½ cup chopped walnuts

Steps

1. **Preheat** the oven to 325°F.

2. Spray the muffin tin with cooking spray.

3. Ask an adult to open the can of pumpkin.

4. Put all the ingredients listed above (except the cooking spray) in the large bowl. **Beat** them together with the mixing spoon until well blended.

5. Spoon the mixture into the muffin tins, filling each compartment ¾ full.

6. Cook regular-size muffins 35 to 40 minutes. Cook mini muffins for 25 minutes.

7. After carefully removing the muffin tin from the oven with the pot holders, let the muffins cool for 5 minutes.

8. Remove the muffins from the tin and eat warm.

Pumpkins are usually yellow or orange but can be dark to pale green, orange-yellow, white, red, or gray.

Baked Stuffed Apples

15 Minutes Prep Time

20 Minutes Cooking Time

Tools

6 Servings

Ingredients

Butter or cooking spray to grease the baking sheet

6 large apples

½ cup chopped walnuts

½ cup dried cranberries or raisins

4 teaspoons maple syrup

1 teaspoon cinnamon

1 teaspoon nutmeg

4 teaspoons butter

Steps

1. **Preheat** the oven to 350°F. Grease the baking sheet.

2. Have an adult remove the cores from the apples with the knife and throw them away.

3. Place the cored apples on the baking sheet.

4. In a small bowl, combine the walnuts, cranberries or raisins, maple syrup, cinnamon, and nutmeg with the mixing spoon.

5. Place the butter in another small bowl and microwave on high for 20 seconds or until melted.

6. Stir the butter into the nut mixture with the mixing spoon.

7. With the spoon, fill the center of the apples with the mixture.

8. Bake in the oven for 20 minutes.

9. Carefully remove the baking sheet from the oven with the pot holders.

10. Let the apples cool for 10 minutes and then enjoy!

Health Tip

At room temperature, an apple will ripen 6 to 10 times faster than in the refrigerator.

The science of growing apples is called pomology. The French word for apple is pomme.

Healthy Tips

Always Read Labels

Labels tell how much fat, sugar, **vitamins**, and other nutrients are in food. If you compare one bottle of juice with another, for example, you can determine which one has fewer **calories**, less sugar, and so on. Don't forget to look at the serving size when comparing foods.

Make Recipe Substitutions

While all the recipes in this book call for wholesome ingredients, you can make even healthier snacks by substituting some ingredients for others. For example:

- Dairy: use nonfat or **low-fat** instead of full fat when it comes to dairy products such as yogurt, cheese, sour cream, and milk.

- Salt: choose "lightly salted" or "no salt added" crackers and pretzels to reduce **sodium** content.

- Juice: choose 100 percent fruit juice or cider with no added sugar.

- Sugar: use honey or agave instead of sugar.

- Flour: use whole wheat flour instead of white flour.

- Butter: use Earth Balance spread or similarly healthy butter in baking instead of real butter.

Nutrition Facts
Serving Size 1 Container (2)0g)
Amount Per Serving
Calories 150   Calories from Fa
% Daily Value*
Total Fat 4g
   Sat. Fat 3g
   Trans Fat 0g
Cholestrerol 10mg
Sodium 65mg
Carbohydrate 8g
   Fiber
   Sugars
Protein 20g
Vitamin A 2% Vitamin C 0% • Calcium 20% • Iron 0%
*Percent Daily Values (DV) are based on a 2,000 calorie

Glossary

antioxidants (*an*-tee-OK-suh-duhnts) substances found in certain foods that may prevent cell damage, which can cause disease in people and animals

beat (BEET) to stir vigorously

blend (BLEND) to mix two or more ingredients together

calories (KAL-uh-reez) measurements of the amount of energy that food provides

cholesterol (kuh-LESS-tuh-*rol*) a fatty substance people need to digest food; too much in the blood can increase the chance of heart disease

core (KOR) the hard center of an apple, pear, or other fruit where the seeds are found

creamy (KREEM-y) something that looks like cream in color and texture

dairy free (DARE-ee FREE) an item that does not contain any milk products

fiber (FYE-bur) a substance found in parts of plants that when eaten passes through the body but is not completely digested; it helps food move through one's intestines and is important for good health

foamy (FOHM-ee) covered with small bubbles

fold (FOHLD) to mix using a gentle turning motion

gluten free (GLOO-tin FREE) an item that does not contain the substance gluten, which is found in wheat, barley, and rye

hulled (HULLED) a seed or fruit that has had its outer covering removed

kernels (KER-nuls) uncooked pieces of corn

low-fat (*loh*-FAT) food that has three or fewer grams of fat per serving

minerals (MIN-ur-uhlz) parts of foods, such as calcium and iron, that a person's body needs to grow and stay healthy

preheat (PREE-heet) to turn on an oven and allow it to heat up to a specific temperature before using

pre-made (PREE-mayd) already prepared

preserve (PREE-zerv) to treat food with something, such as a chemical, so that it doesn't spoil

produce (PROH-doos) things that have been grown, especially by farming

roast (ROHST) to cook in a hot oven

sauté (saw-TAY) to fry in a small amount of fat

simmer (SIM-ur) to boil slowly at a low temperature

sodium (SOH-dee-uhm) a chemical found in salt that the body needs in small amounts; too much salt in one's diet can cause health problems

vegan (VEE-gin) a diet that contains no animal food or dairy products

vitamins (VYE-tuh-minz) substances in food that are necessary for good health

Index

Bibliography

Beery, Barbara. *Fairies Cookbook*. Layton, Utah: Gibbs Smith (2007).

D'Amico, Joan, and Karen Eich Drummond. *The Healthy Body Cookbook*. New York: John Wiley (1999).

Read More

Graimes, Nicola. *Kids' Fun and Healthy Cookbook*. New York: Dorling Kindersley (2007).

Low, Jennifer. *Kitchen for Kids: 100 Amazing Recipes Your Children Can Really Make*. Canada: Whitecap Books (2010).

Learn More Online

To learn more about making cool drinks and snacks, visit
www.bearportpublishing.com/YummyTummy-Seasons

About the Author

Marilyn LaPenta has been a teacher for more than 25 years and has published numerous works for teachers and students. She has always enjoyed cooking with her students and her three children, and looks forward to cooking with her three grandchildren. Marilyn lives in Brightwaters, New York.